COACHING MATCHUP DEFENSE

PRESSURE DEFENSIVE PHILOSOPHIES

Bob Huggins

D1605307

ISBN: 1-58518-175-7

Cover Design: Charles L. Peters
Interior Design: Janet Wahlfeldt
Cover Photos: Brian Spurlock
Editor: David Hamburg

Coaches Choice Books is a division of: Coaches Choice
P.O. Box 1828
Monterey, CA 93942
Web Site: http://www.coacheschoiceweb.com

CONTENTS

Introduction 4

Overview 5

Diagram Key 8

Chapter

1   The 1-1-3 Matchup 9

2   The 1-2-2 Matchup 49

3   Drilling the Fundamentals of the Matchup............................ 59

4   Making Adjustments from Your Matchup Zone 71

5   Checklist to Evaluate Your Matchup 77

Conclusion 79

About the Author 80

INTRODUCTION

Thanks for taking the time to read this book on coaching the matchup defense. While the book doesn't contain the answers for stopping every type of offense, it does provide a variety of ideas from which you can choose. In deciding which style of defense to play, a coach must evaluate not only the players on his team, but also the athletes he is going to be competing against. The matchup defense is the cornerstone of the defensive schemes that we used at the University of Cincinnati.

Success in basketball comes through drills and repetition—not game-night heroics. The skills achieved by individual players must be perfected through practice habits. Most coaches will agree that man-to-man defense is the most effective defense in basketball, especially if the athletes you are working with are superior to your opponents in quickness, agility and strength. As aggressive man-to-man defenses have become more popular, man-to-man offenses have also improved. Each year, most coaches begin with offensive practices that emphasize their man-to-man attack; they almost always spend more time on those offenses than the ones designed to counter other defenses.

After you have coached a short time, you will realize that you will not always have superior talent and therefore will not consistently be able to control and dominate each opponent with your man-to-man defense. Your choices then become the following: to have a secondary defensive strategy using a zone, a combination of zone and man or a matchup defense. Although standard zone defenses offer a change-up in most situations, the weaknesses of the seams, gaps and defensive block-outs provide a solution that usually takes a superior team a few possessions to exploit. Add to that the ability of modern shooters to score easily from the three-point line, and most pure zones will lose their effectiveness quickly.

Combination defenses (e.g., triangle-and-two, box-and-one, diamond-and-one) often are effective in briefly stopping the best players on opposing teams. Seldom, however, are they solid enough to provide sufficient coverage for any appreciable length of time, and they often leave the defense as confused as the offense. The matchup defense can be used as a primary defense. It is capable of successfully defending a strong opponent for an entire game, as well as creating turnovers and disrupting offenses at every level. This book will introduce you to a variety of alignments that can be used to teach the matchup. It will become your job to choose the one that best fits your personnel. The four main formations that we will focus on will be the 1-1-3, the 1-3-1, the 2-1-2 and the 1-2-2. The strengths and weaknesses of each formation will be spelled out in detail to assist you in deciding which formation will best suit your team. In addition, drills are included so you can take the information directly from the book and into your practice session. I hope these defensive concepts will be helpful to your team and coaching staff and be as successful for you as they have been for us.

OVERVIEW

The matchup defense combines the best principles of both man-to-man and zone defenses into one concept. In the matchup, each defender is responsible for playing man-to-man on the player(s) in his area of the floor. By matching the original alignment of the offensive team, the defensive team can stay in man-to-man if the offensive team is content to move the ball as if it is playing against a zone. As soon as the offense adds cutting and player movement, then the defense begins using the principle of "passing, or releasing," the cutters to the next defensive player as the offensive players move through his zone.

For the teams that treat the matchup as a zone, we counter by using more of the man-to-man principles of the matchup. Against teams that attack it by using more man-to-man offensive movement and screens, we emphasize the zone concepts of the matchup. Each of these maneuvers exploits the strengths of the defense against the weaknesses of the offense. As offensive teams improve their screening, cutting and reading in "passing game," pattern play and terminal action play offenses, your straight man-to-man defenses are severely tested, both collectively and individually. The matchup is effective against all of these types of offenses. In order to compete against your defense, opposing teams are often forced into making special preparations that they do not have to make for any other opponent. Few coaches have enough practice time to devote to "specialized offenses" and therefore either don't give it as much time or simply try to run what they already can do against your "specialized defense." Advantage to the defense.

As with the man-to-man, the matchup allows you to hide a weak defender or a player in foul trouble in order to protect him. Similar to a zone, the matchup allows you to focus on an outstanding offensive player by placing your best defenders in the areas where your opponent is the most effective, while giving more space to those who cannot hurt you. The matchup also provides you with the opportunity to leave your better rebounders close to the basket.

The initial alignment you choose in your matchup can also determine the type of alignment the offensive team will use to attack it. This knowledge will allow you to predict—and therefore prepare for—your opponent's specific type of offensive set. In general, odd-front defenses will be attacked by an even-front offense, and a two-guard front on defense will most often see a single-guard offensive set. As a coach in this situation, you can determine which of their attacks is the weakest and force them into playing that set. For example, if their two-guard-front offense is not as effective as some others, you can force their hand by coming out in a 1-3-1 or 1-2-2 matchup.

In order to best prepare your matchup, you must do an excellent job of scouting. This will allow you not only to identify the strongest players and where they like to operate, but more important, their basic cuts and screens. Understanding ahead of time what your opponents like to do when they face man or zone will allow you to match up and neutralize their strengths from the first possession.

Another advantage of solid defense is the ability to control the tempo of the game. Most offensive teams concede that it takes longer to attack a zone defense, and the same is true of the matchup. By forcing teams to make extra passes in an attempt to find an open shot, the defense can force the offense into more turnovers and violations. This usually results in fast breaks for your team and also causes the offense to become even more conservative than it is. The matchup becomes even more effective against a team playing from behind and having to score quickly.

The man-to-man features of the matchup allow you to have each offensive player checked, with help always close by, thereby eliminating the effectiveness of dribble penetration. The zone features of the matchup neutralize screens on the ball or away from the ball. The matchup is always in position to sag and help on an outstanding offensive post player, thus eliminating the chance of one player beating you.

Every coach has to establish his own defensive scheme that revolves around his knowledge and the abilities of his players. Even if you do not use the matchup in your defensive system, you will have to play against it sometime during the season. The better you can understand it, the more effective you can be as either an offensive or a defensive coach.

In summary, we choose to play the matchup for the following reasons:

- It neutralizes superior talent.

- It causes opposing teams to make special preparations for our defense.

- It makes opponents tentative and unsure.

- It is effective with small or slow players—if they are smart.

- It incorporates the strengths of both man and zone defenses.

- It uses most of the defensive concepts of our man-to-man.

- Depending on the front we choose to show, it enables us to force the offense into specific formations.

- It gives the coach the ability to hide or protect individual players.

- It keeps our rebounders in the proper position.

- By scouting, we can prepare for all the specific cuts and screens.

- It controls the tempo of the game by making the offense take longer to attack than it would like to, yet it still provides fast-break opportunities.

- It neutralizes screening and penetration as offensive weapons.

- It allows us to contain a strong offensive individual, whether he is a post player or a perimeter player.

- It can be adapted to a full-court pressing scheme.

- It can be used to defend baseline, out-of-bounds situations.

DIAGRAM KEY

COACH = **C**

OFFENSIVE PLAYER = ○

SPECIFIC OFFENSIVE PLAYERS = ① ② ③ ④ ⑤

OFFENSIVE PLAYER WITH THE BALL = ○•

DEFENSIVE PLAYER = X

SPECIFIC DEFENSIVE PLAYERS = X_1 X_2 X_3 X_4 X_5

PASS = - - - ->

CUT OR PATH OF THE PLAYER = ———>

DRIBBLER = ~~~~

SCREEN = ——|

OFFENSIVE PLAYER O4 WHO STARTS WITH THE BALL, PASSES IT TO O2 AND THEN SCREENS FOR O3, WHO USES HIS SCREEN TO CUT

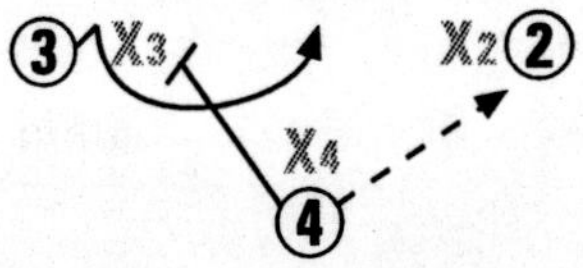

The 1-1-3 Matchup

THE 1-1-3 MATCH UP ZONE

We have run this particular type of matchup for the last 15 years. This is the first defense we will teach after our man-to-man has been installed, because, as you will see, it uses most of the same techniques and terminology as our man defense. This defense has been effective regardless of the differences in our personnel from year to year. Even when our teams have possessed a lot of quickness or athleticism, we have had success with the 1-1-3 matchup. It has proven to be a disruptive defense at every level.

We coach the game from the perspective of simply trying to get more and better shots than our opponent. The 1-1-3 matchup helps by creating turnovers, thus allowing us to score off our defense in transition. It has helped limit our opponents' field goal percentage, because shots are usually taken off the dribble, and we are in excellent rebounding position. Creating the illusion that people are open and then rotating to the openings and shooting the gaps before the ball gets there causes turnovers.

This chapter will focus on the following areas:

- The general alignment

- The box theory

- Positions

- Drills

- Responsibilities by position

- Up the line, on the line

- Rotations

- Keys to success for the 1-1-3 matchup

GENERAL ALIGNMENT OF THE 1-1-3

Diagram 1 shows the basic alignment of the 1-1-3 matchup. It represents our initial lineup of personnel. It is important that each of our players knows who he is guarding. He may be responsible for a player he does not originally line up next to. A good offense will attempt to distort the defense with its offensive alignment. We want our players to know who they are guarding without getting distorted.

From here we use the philosophy of the box theory the same as we do in our man-to-man defense. By keeping the theories the same, the players have a quicker carryover into this particular matchup. The simpler we can make the transition from man-to-man to matchup, the better our players understand the defense and the quicker they can become aggressive as a team.

Diagram 1

THE BOX THEORY

A few years ago, when we had our practice time reduced, we became very concerned that we would not have enough time to teach everything that we do. By examining our practice schedules from past years, we evaluated everything we did and why we did it. We took a fresh look at every drill and technique to see if it fit into our general philosophy about how we felt the game should be played.

Not only had the amount of practice time changed, but in some ways the game had also changed. With increased athleticism, some of the fundamentals and theories we had always used were becoming outdated or not applicable to our present thinking. One of those areas we had to rethink was denying the wing pass. The only rationale I could come up with for continuing to require that we deny the wing was that we had always done it that way. When I began playing basketball, the dominant defensive philosophy was to force the ball into the middle of the floor, where all the help was located. We protected the lane area with our help-side people, keeping the big people home and funneling everything into them. With this philosophy, it made perfect sense to keep the ball off the side of the floor; therefore, denying the wing was a sound defensive concept.

Since we have changed our philosophy to pushing the ball to the side by either the pass or the dribble, denying the wing pass keeps the ball from where we want it to go in the first place. Therefore, we no longer deny any pass to the wing or the corner; we simply try to make the offensive player catch the ball while going away from the basket.

The following pages describe the "box theory" and our attempt to push the ball further and further into the corner so we have less and less court to try to defend.

Our matchup defense is based on the box theory: the court is divided into two boxes, depending on where the ball is located.

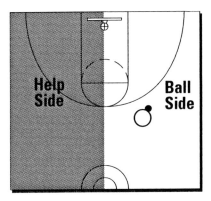

Diagram 2

We attempt to put the ball into one box on the ball side and keep it there. We do not deny any pass going deeper in the box. In fact, we encourage those passes, as long as the offensive player is moving away from the basket as he catches the pass.

Diagram 3

We will deny any pass that makes the box larger. X1 denies the ball back to the wing, once it has been pushed into the corner in Diagram 4. X2 denies the ball into the high post from the corner. Each of these passes would have increased the size of the box. All of our denial drill now revolves around keeping the ball in the box and keeping the box as small as possible.

Diagram 4

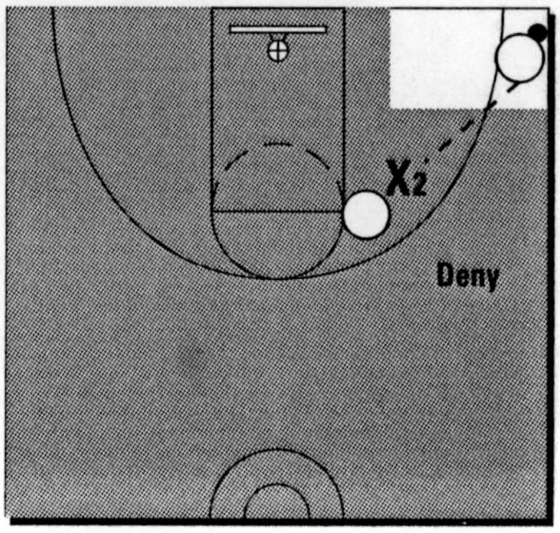

Diagram 5

We must deny even harder any pass that would make us change sides of the court and, therefore, make us change boxes.

Diagram 6

Diagram 7

We encourage the ball to be passed further into the box because it then shortens the area that we have to guard. All of our defenders must be close enough so that with one big step, they can have one foot in the box.

Diagram 8

As this diagram shows, the box is on the ball side of the court and level with the ball. All the defenders are close enough to take one big step and get a foot in the box. The deeper the ball is penetrated, the smaller the box becomes and the closer each defender gets to the man with the ball.

Diagram 9

ON THE LINE, UP THE LINE

In order to play the box correctly, our players must be able to defend potential receivers who would increase the size of the box if they caught the ball. To deny these players the ball, we require that our defenders understand the concept of *on the line, up the line.* This term is used to describe the position of the player guarding a man off the ball. The defender off the ball must be in a direct line between his man and the ball. Being in the on-the-line, up-the-line position does the following things for our team defense:

- It takes away the vision from the offense. Anytime we can take away the vision of the offense, it increases our chances of causing turnovers and being successful.

- It discourages skip passes because the man is harder to find and our defender can intercept the pass much more easily.

- It makes it much easier to teach the trap when you decide to add trapping to either your half-court or full-court matchup defense.

Example of *on the line, up the line* with the ball at the point.

Diagram 10

In the examples diagrammed, notice that all the players are directly on the line of the ball and up the line toward the ball. How far they move up the line depends not only on how quick they are, but also on how quick their opponent is. The quicker you are than your opponent, the further off him you may come toward the ball. Because of the varying degrees of quickness among basketball players, all players would not be in the same place up the line, but all would stay on the line.

Example of *on the line, up the line* with the ball on the wing.

Diagram 11

Example of *on the line, up the line* with the ball in the corner.

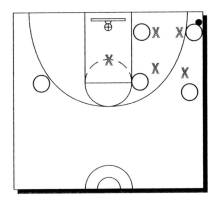

Diagram 12

The on-the-line, up-the-line theory is in contrast to the more common theory of being in a flat triangle position. The *flat triangle theory* places the player in off-the-ball defense in a position one step off the direct line toward the basket.

Example of the *flat triangle* position.

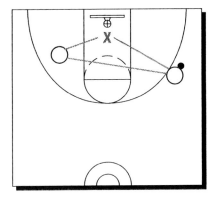

Diagram 13

As you can see, the defender is closer to the basket than if he were playing on the line, up the line. The point of the triangle would be the defender, with the base of the triangle being the ball at one end and the man being guarded at the other.

Example of team defensive positions in the flat triangle with the ball on the wing.

Diagram 14

The flat triangle method of positioning the defender the off the ball is a sound defensive philosophy, but we do not feel that you can cause as much disruption from this position as you can by being directly on the line. The major reason I feel that most coaches teach the flat triangle position is that the defender does not have to turn his head to see both the ball and his man. I agree with them, as long as both the ball and (or) your man never move. Since all offenses involve both player and ball movement, the defenders constantly have to turn their heads in order to keep track of one or the other. The same is true of being on the line, up the line; and since it is a more aggressive position, we choose to teach this theory.

A number of drills can be used to teach the defender to stay in an on-the-line, up-the-line position and work on his vision (Diagrams 15-24). As shown in Diagram 15,this drill helps the player stay in an on-the-line, up-the-line position with the ball moving. The coach has the ball, and he moves so the defender must adjust his position in order to stay on the line. The offensive player remains stationary. This drill should be done in a different spot on the floor when it is repeated.

Diagram 15

This drill begins with the defender in an on-the-line, up-the-line position and the coach with the ball. The coach remains stationary while the offensive player without the ball moves in and out towards the basket and closer or further from the ball.

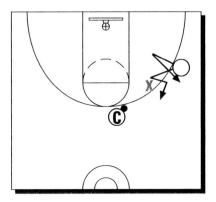

Diagram 16

In this drill, the defender begins in an on-the-line, up-the-line position between the ball and his man. The coach with the ball and the player without the ball both move so the defender gets a more game-like movement. The defender attempts to keep his position while seeing both the ball and his man. All of these drills can start with slow-motion movement and then gradually increase in speed.

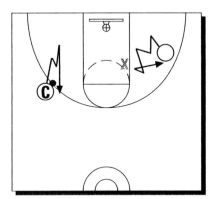

Diagram 17

Another technique that helps our players play on the line, up the line is called *sprint to help*. This technique allows the defender to go from a position on the ball to an on-the-line, up-the-line position when his man passes the ball. After your man has passed the ball, the natural tendency is either to relax or to drop toward the basket rather than to the ball. The defender must stay in his stance and immediately jump to the ball while he stays in line. How far he moves toward the ball is again based upon his quickness relative to his opponent's.

One drill that is designed to master this technique is called *sprint to help* with the ball passed across the key. This drill begins with the defender on the ball, two steps off the elbow. The offensive player passes the ball to the opposite wing. As the ball is in the air, the defender must sprint to the middle of the floor so he can be close enough to the newly established box that he can take one large step and have a foot in the box. The defender positions himself not only to be off his man, but also to be on the. It is important that he get off his man quickly so he is between his man and the ball; that way, he is not beaten on a direct cut to the basket, and, as a result, he can be in a position to help on any dribble penetration.

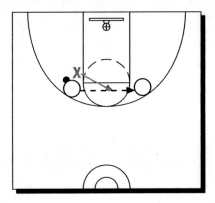

Diagram 18

The sprint-to-help drill should be practiced at a variety of places on the court so that it becomes instinctive for your defensive players to immediately move to the correct position after their offensive man has passed the ball. In Diagram 19, for example, the ball is passed from the wing to the corner, and X1 sprints to help.

Diagram 19

Diagram 20 shows the setup for a three-on-two sprint-to-help drill. Offensive players set up on each wing and are defended by X1 and X2, who are in an on-the-line, up-the-line position. The coach stands unguarded at the top of the circle and begins the drill with the ball.

Diagram 20

Three-on-two sprint to help drill. The defenders allow the ball to be caught, even though they are in an on-the-line, up-the-line position. As the coach passes the ball to the left wing, the defender away from the wing (X2) sprints to help, assuming the correct position.

Diagram 21

As the ball is passed back to the coach at the top of the circle, both defenders jump back to their original positions of on the line, up the line, able to deny a direct pass to their man.

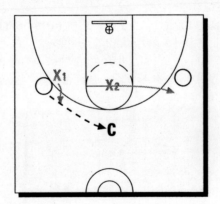

Diagram 22

The sprint-to-help drill continues as the ball is reversed through the coach and to the right wing, causing X1 to be in the sprint-to-help position, close enough to be within one step of having a foot in the box. Keep reversing the ball through the coach to give the players enough repetitions in the proper on-the-line, up-the-line techniques.

Diagram 23

This drill is the same three-on-two sprint-to-help drill, but on the side of the court.

Diagram 24

PISTOLS POSITION

The term we use to describe the correct hand position assumed by the defender off the ball is the *pistols position*. When the defender is in an on-the-line, up-the-line position, his stance is open, meaning that he is open to the ball and to his man. Both toes would be directly on the imaginary line between the ball and the offensive man he is defending.

The term "pistols" comes from the position the defender holds his hands in while he is in a defensive stance. With one index finger, he is pointing at the ball, and with the other index finger, he is pointing at the man he is defending. His hands will thus look like two pistols pointing in different directions. This technique is the one we require for the defender so he can keep track of the movement of both the ball and his man. When a defender is off the ball, his hands should never be down, but rather always out to the side of his body and pointed purposefully toward the ball and his man. A coach may be able to determine when a defender is tired by observing his pistols position, and can always tell if the player has lost track of either the ball or his man by the position of his hands.

Having the arms away from the body allows the defender to meet and shed potential screens and not let the screener get to his body. A good screener is going to attempt to get solid contact with the shoulder and legs of his opponent, but by keeping his pistols out to the side of his body, the defender makes first contact with his hands when he is being screened. Besides having his pistols out and pointing, the off-the-ball defender should never come out of his stance. He should play with his knees bent and his hips down to increase his quickness. This athletic position is the same one used in almost any sport when quick movement is required.

Off-the-ball defenders are also required to be turning their heads constantly to see not only the ball and their man, but also to see if any screeners are approaching. We also want our off-the-ball defenders in a *pistols position* so they can see where everyone is on the floor in order to make straight-line rotations. We try to drop in a straight line to the man we are rotating to—and having vision is the key.

PLAYER RESPONSIBILITIES AND DESCRIPTIONS

As we start to build the matchup zone, we must identify the different positions and responsibilities that come with each one. In order to have a sound defensive team, we must place our players in the proper position on the floor to give them a chance for success. The following are the five positions and a general idea of where we place our players. You may have to evaluate your own personnel and make some adjustments to ensure that they have the physical abilities required to play these positions.

- **1 man**—Generally, the smaller of the two guards, and usually, our offensive point man.

- **2 man**—The better defensive player of the two guards. If they are even defensively, then place the better athlete in this spot.

- **3 man**—He is our small forward, usually our frontline player with the quickest feet and our most aggressive on-the-ball defender. He may be your third guard if you run a three-guard offense in high school.

- **4 man**—He is generally the second-quickest defender of our frontline players, and he is also an active, aggressive rebounder.

- **5 man**—This is the spot where we place our biggest and least active inside player. His most important jobs are to protect the basket, front the low post and rebound aggressively.

Both the guard positions and all three forward positions are interchangeable. Consequently, if you have players who are all equal athletically, it is to your advantage. Guards must learn to play both guard positions, and the big people must learn the slides for all three inside positions in order for your team to be successful. Next, we will look at the specific responsibilities by position.

GENERAL RESPONSIBILITIES OF THE GUARDS

As we cover the responsibilities of the guards, we need to keep in mind how the guards relate to the overall scheme of the defense. The guards are basically responsible for every pass that goes away from the basket. The only penetrating pass that they cannot allow is the one to the high post. Other than that pass, they do not deny any passes that go closer to the baseline. The guards work as though a pulley is connecting them. One of the guards is always in the high post area, while the other is on the perimeter. They are never both in the high post or both on the perimeter at the same time. This technique enables us to do a better job of keeping the ball in the box. Since both guards are responsible for defending all passes away from the basket, they are basically keeping the ball from leaving and enlarging the box. If they are successful at their jobs, the guards will also keep the ball from changing sides of the floor, which forces us to change boxes.

Diagram 25 shows the initial setup of the two guards, keeping in mind the general responsibilities described above.

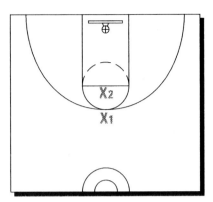

Diagram 25

SPECIFIC RESPONSIBILITIES OF THE GUARDS

X1

Diagram 26 shows the drill we use to teach X1 to control the ball, get it out of the center, and then deny the return pass to the point guard.

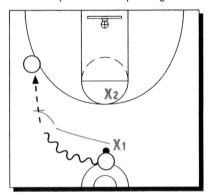

Diagram 26

X1

- He must get the ball under control. Ideally, he should be able to "flatten out" the dribbler, making him go parallel to the half-court line.

- He must not let the ball be centered in the middle of the floor so they can begin their offense.

- He influences the ball to one side of the floor or the other and keeps it on that side so the box is established.

- He must pressure the ball—not allowing passes to go uncontested. Ideally, he works for deflections on the entry pass.

- Once the point guard passes the ball, he must deny the reversal pass back to the point guard. Keep in mind that both guards allow passes that penetrate (except the high post) and take away all passes that go away from the basket.

X2

This diagram shows X2 in his initial position. He must drill on defending players already in the high post when the ball is brought down the court, and then switching to a three-quarter position when the ball goes below the foul line.

Diagram 27

X2

- He must keep the ball out of the high post. In order to do that effectively, if someone begins in the high post area, he must be in a denial stance. If no one is in the high post, he must have vision toward the key area of the court so that cutters don't flash into the high post without his being aware that they are approaching.

- If no one is playing in the high post area initially, he must sink and find the first cutter into the high post.

- He must keep his head moving so he can have vision of players from both sides of the court who could potentially flash into the high post area of the court.

- When a player is located in the high post, he uses a full front position if the ball is above the foul line and a three-quarter denial stance on the low side if the ball is below the foul line.

Diagram 28 illustrates the drill we use to work on X2's technique in denying the ball to players flashing into the high post. Remember that if no one is in the high post initially, then he must sink and find the first cutter into that area.

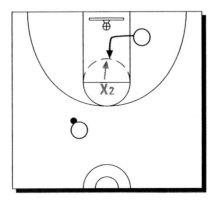

Diagram 28

In this drill, X2 keeps his head moving so that he is aware of any players who may cut into the high post area from the wings. We will place two potential cutters on the weak side and alternately flash them into the high post so that X2 can meet and deny them the ball.

Diagram 29

GENERAL RESPONSIBILITIES OF THE FORWARDS

As we cover the responsibilities of the forwards, it should be kept in mind how their jobs relate to the overall scheme of the defense. Each forward's main objective is to take away all penetrating passes toward the basket. Once the forward has closed out on the first pass to the wing, he attempts to force the ball to be dribbled or passed to the baseline. He cannot allow any dribble penetration to the middle of the floor. Everything must be pushed toward the baseline, which will continue to make the box smaller.

In order to be effective at these responsibilities (Note: Remember that the X3, X4 and X5 positions are interchangeable), the forwards must have the following defensive skills:

- effective closeout techniques

- proper footwork to stop the dribbler

- active feet and hands so that they are able to front cutters and posts in the center of the floor

Diagram 30 shows the initial setup for the forwards in our matchup.

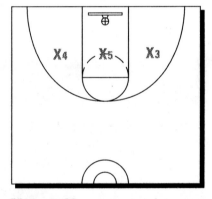

Diagram 30

SPECIFIC RESPONSIBILITIES OF THE FORWARDS

X3
- Since most players are right-handed, X3 is usually the ball-side forward.

- Closes out on the first penetrating pass, trying to make the offensive player move away from the basket as he catches the ball.

- Closes out on the high side with "high hands" to force the ball toward the baseline.

- Cannot allow the ball to be penetrated to the middle of the floor by the dribble.

- Tries to make the wing dribble, but always toward the baseline.

- Tries to take away the vision of the offensive player

X5

- He is the middle man on the matchup.

- Fronts any low-block player, keeping the ball from going toward the basket when the ball is passed to the wing.

- He cannot get caught behind the post, or he will not be able to make the next rotation when the ball is passed to the corner.

X4

- He is the offside forward if the ball is entered away from him.

- He must be close enough to be within one step of the box.

- He is on the line, up the line with his man in the matchup.

- He is the last line of defense.

- He is the backside help on the fronted post and the weakside rebounder.

- He is anchored on this side of the court for a purpose, and we never try to rotate him all the way across the floor.

ROTATIONS

In order to correctly play the matchup, it is essential that all players understand and execute the rotations required to remain within the rules of the defense. Correct rotations are dependent on the location of the offensive players and the ball. In the following descriptions, I will identify the rotations for the guards and the forwards that are based upon these factors.

The most vulnerable area of any zone is the high post. Most of the rules for rotation by both the guards and the forwards depend on whether the offensive team has a man in the high post area. If the ball gets entered into the high post, all the other four offensive players are potential receivers, and therefore the defense will be severely tested. All areas of the court are open to pass into and the concept of keeping the ball in a continuously shrinking box becomes very difficult. The offensive player in the high post must be defended in such a way that he is denied the ball at all times by the rotation of the defensive players. All defensive players must move while the ball is traveling in the air so that they have made the proper rotation and are already in the new location as the ball is caught.

Good defensive players away from the ball must be aware of the man they are responsible for and the location of the ball. In addition, they must use their peripheral vision and constant foot movement in order to be ready to make any rotations necessary for team coverage. They must also use their voices to alert teammates to players entering into their area who could determine the next rotation. After making a shift, each player should stay with that man until offensive-player or ball movement dictates the next rotation. The defensive team must move as a unit, with each player moving in the direction of the pass before his man does.

The basic premise of this defense is that no matter what defense you play, it is still a five-on-five game (one defender for every offensive player), and everyone should always have a man. Our players should never get caught "guarding air" or a spot on the floor. To my knowledge, a spot on the floor has never scored a point in the game of basketball.

GUARD ROTATION ON THE INITIAL PASS TO THE WING—OFFENSIVE MAN IN THE HIGH POST

Diagram 31

X1

- Starts on the ball and then jumps in the direction of the pass in order to stay on the line and up the line

- Denies the pass back to the point

- He must move while the ball is in the air so that he is in the proper position by the time the ball is caught on the wing

X2

- Begins in a denial position on the high post with the ball on the point and then jumps to the ball side of the high post as the ball is in the air

- Gets into a three-quarter-front position on the low side of the high post. His outside foot should be up above the level of the offensive high post, and his outside hand should be in a position to deny a direct pass

- From this position, he needs to be ready to support the wing defender in case he gets beaten to the middle of the floor

DRILL TO TEACH GUARD ROTATION ON A WING PASS WITH A HIGH POST

The coach begins with the ball at the point defended by X1 and passes the ball to the wing. A third offensive player positions himself at the high post. The two defenders (X1 and X2) must make the correct rotations on the pass in order to deny the ball to the post or back to the point. Since the guards need to know both positions, they should drill in both places.

Diagram 32

X1
- Starts on the coach with the ball, attempting to influence him toward one side of the court and pressure the passer.

- As the ball is passed to the wing, jumps in a direct on-the-line, up-the-line position and denies the ball back to the point

X2
- Begins in a denial position or by being in a three-quarter-front position around on the inside of the post

- As the ball is passed, jumps in the direction of the pass and three-quarter fronts the post on the ball side

- Cannot get pinned on the inside by the post, uses quick foot movement to get around to the ball side

ROTATION BY THE FORWARDS ON THE INITIAL PASS TO THE WING – OFFENSIVE MAN IN THE HIGH POST (DIAGRAM 33)

Diagram 33

X3

- Ball-side forward

- Rotates to take the man receiving the first penetrating pass on his side

- Closes out on the high side, with hands high, forcing the ball to be driven or passed to the baseline, therefore shortening the box

- Pressures the ball to affect the vision of the offensive player

- Tries to force the player to dribble

X4

- Offside forward

- Stays on a line between the ball and his man and assumes the pistols position

- Acts as the weakside rebounder in case of a shot

X5

- Matches up with anyone in the low-block area, basket out

- Full fronts a low post

- If no offensive players are in the low post, takes the next man across the lane

DRILL TO TEACH FORWARD ROTATION ON THE INITIAL WING PASS WITH AN OFFENSIVE PLAYER IN THE HIGH POST.

The coach starts with the ball on the point and can enter the ball to either wing. Defensive forwards start in their initial positions and react with the correct rotation, depending on which side the coach enters the ball. An offensive player is in the high post, even though the forwards do not have responsibility for him, and there is a low post player who can move toward the ball side or stay opposite.

In Diagram 34, the coach enters the ball to O2, making X3 the ball-side forward who closes out on the high side, forcing the dribbler to the baseline. X5 fronts the low post player if he comes to the block, or else X5 gets into an on-the-line, up-the-line position if the low post player stays across the lane. X4 gets on the line, up the line with O3 and rebounds weakside on any shot.

In Diagram 35, the coach enters the ball to O3, and X4 then becomes the ball-side forward and closes out on the high side. X5 fronts the low post player or gets into a pistols position if the low post player stays opposite. X3 gets on the line, up the line with the remaining player on the weak side of the floor.

Diagram 34

Diagram 35

GUARD POTATIONS FOR THE SECOND PASS, BALL SIDE, TO THE CORNER–OFFENSIVE PLAYER IN THE HIGH POST

Diagram 36

X1

- From the position of being on the line, up the line with the wing, dives into the high post on the ball side

- Guards the man in the high post in an on-the-line, up-the-line position

- As he dives to the high post, "bumps" or "releases" X1 to the wing

- Covers the low post if O4 drives to the basket

X2

- Keeps guarding the high post until X1 gets there, and then he bumps out to the wing to deny the pass back out to the wing

- If no player is on the wing, defends the next closest player from receiving a pass out of the corner

- On a penetrating dribble that pulls X1 out of the high post, splits the wing and high post and anticipates the steal

FORWARD ROTATIONS FOR THE SECOND PASS, BALL SIDE, TO THE CORNER—OFFENSIVE PLAYER IN THE HIGH POST

Diagram 37

X3

- On the ball, sprints directly to the man in the low post while the ball is in the air

- Should have a maximum of three steps in which to get to the low post (run, don't shuffle)

- If no one is in the low post, guards the next man over and bumps X4 up

- Could also drop to the medium post, if the low post steps up the lane

X4

- Serves as our "anchor man" as the weakside defender

- Has weakside rebounding responsibility, and he also supports the low post if necessary

- Stays on the line, up the line with any offensive player in his box

X5

- Leaves the low post as the ball is in the air

- Attacks the man in the corner head up and hands high

- Influences the offensive man to the baseline with his closeout and tries never to let the ball get penetrated to the middle of the floor

ROTATIONS FOR GUARDS AND FORWARDS COMBINED FOR SECOND PASS, BALL SIDE, TO THE CORNER—OFFENSIVE PLAYER IN THE HIGH POST

O3 starts with the ball on the wing and passes to O4 in the corner. X1, X2, X3 and X4 must move to the proper position as the ball is in the air:

Diagram 38

X1
- Dives to the high post and guards the offensive high post in an up-the-line, on-the-line position

X2
- Gets bumped to the wing and denies the pass out of the corner

X3
- Sprints from the ball to the low post

X4
- Remains as the weakside defender and rebounder who can help at the low post

X5
- Closes out on the man receiving the ball in the corner and influences him toward the baseline

DRILL TO COMBINE THE FIRST TWO PASSES (POINT TO WING AND WING TO CORNER) AND THE ROTATIONS OF BOTH GUARDS AND FORWARDS— OFFENSIVE PLAYER AT THE HIGH POST

This drill combines the rotations for two consecutive passes. O1 passes the ball to O3 on the wing, who holds the ball for a two-count before passing it to the corner. All defenders must move while the pass is in the air. The players should gradually speed up the timing of the second pass.

Diagram 39

Diagram 40

X1
- Jumps off the ball to an on-the-line position (pass 1) and then sprints to the high post (pass 2)

X2
- Gets around the high post on the ball side (pass 1), then sprints to the wing and denies (pass 2)

X3
- Closes out on the wing (pass 1) and sprints to the low block (pass 2)

X4
- Moves with each pass to adjust his weakside position and help with the low post

X5
- Moves to front the low post (pass 1) and then closes out to the corner (pass 2)

GUARD ROTATIONS FOR A SKIP PASS FROM WING TO WING—OFFENSIVE PLAYER IN THE HIGH POST

This pass should be very difficult to make if the man on the ball is taking away vision with high hands, and the man on the weak side is in the correct on-the-line position. But if the pass is made, the guards must react instinctively.

Diagram 41

X1

- Sprints from an on-the-line, up-the-line position with O1 to the opposite side

- Denies the reversal to the point

- Prepares to dive to the high post on penetration by the wing or a pass to the corner

- Keeps the ball from being centered

X2

- Sprints from one side of the high post to the other, beating him to the ball side

- From the high post denial position prepares either to dive to the low post if the ball is dribble penetrated from the wing, or to get bumped out to the wing if the ball is passed into the corner

FORWARD ROTATIONS FOR A SKIP PASS FROM WING TO WING—OFFENSIVE PLAYER IN THE HIGH POST

Again, this should be a very difficult pass if the man on the ball is taking away the vision of the passer with high hands, and the man on the weak side is in the correct on the line position.

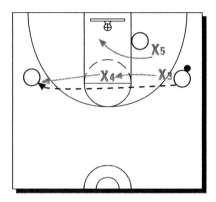

Diagram 42

X3
- Goes from the on-the-ball position to sprint to help, on the line and up the line

- Needs to be close enough to be within a step of the ball-side box

- Stays matched with the man who passed the ball until the offensive players move

X4
- Closes out on the high side of the offensive player receiving the pass

- Closes out with high hands to take away the offensive player's vision

- Tries to force the offense to become a dribbler

- Protects the middle of the floor, forcing toward the baseline

X5
- Sprints from a front position to a help position and stays matched if the post does not cut block to block

- Stays on and up the line, beating the offensive player if he cuts to the ball-side post

DRILL TO COMBINE THE ROTATIONS OF GUARDS AND FORWARDS ON A SKIP PASS FROM THE WING—OFFENSIVE PLAYER IN THE HIGH POST

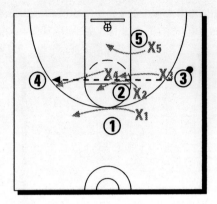

Diagram 43

X1
- Sprints to help as the ball is in the air and denies the reversal pass to the point

X2
- Gets around the high post into a denial position on the ball side

X3
- Sprints to help, on the line and up the line, staying within one step of the ball-side box

X4
- Closes out on the receiver, hands high and on the high side to force him baseline

X5
- Sprints to help around the low post and prepares to beat him to the spot if he cuts block to block

GUARD ROTATIONS FOR THE SKIP PASS FROM WING TO WING—HIGH POST VACANT

With no offensive player in the high post, X2 is matched with O2 on the opposite wing (Diagram 44) and is now responsible for that player when he receives the skip pass.

Diagram 44   **Diagram 45**

X1
- Dives from an on-the-line and up-the-line position, where he was denying the point reversal into the high post, and gets into the pistols position

- Takes any cutter coming into the high post area

- If the ball is passed into the paint, he matches up with the point

- Blocks out the high post on a shot

X2
- Closes out on O2, with hands high to limit his vision, and stays on the high side

- Tries to force the offensive player to dribble

- Protects the middle of the floor, forcing him toward the baseline

FORWARD ROTATIONS FOR THE SKIP PASS FROM WING TO WING—HIGH POST VACANT

Diagram 46

Diagram 47

X3

- From an on-the-ball position, sprints to help and gets into the pistols position

- Matches with the offensive player who just passed the ball

- Now becomes the weakside anchor of the defense and rebounds weakside

- Is close enough to take one step and be in the ball-side box

X4

- Sprints to the ball side of the man he is matched with

- Fronts his man if he is in the low post

- Stays on the line and up the line

- Would take the next pass if the ball is thrown to the corner

- Is ready to help baseline if the offense is driven there

X5

- Sprints to help, ball side

- Is in the pistols position if X4 is still fronting the low post

COMBINED ROTATIONS FOR GUARDS AND FORWARDS FOR A SKIP PASS FROM WING TO WING—HIGH POST VACANT

Diagram 48

X1
- Dives into the high post and takes any cutter into the high post

X2
- Closes out on the receiver (O2) and forces toward the baseline

X3
- Sprints to help, close enough to be one step from the ball-side box

X4
- Sprints to the ball side of his man, fronts the low post or allows his man to catch the ball if he is in the corner

X5
- Sprints to help on the ball side of his man and helps X4, who is fronting the low post on the ball side

CONTINUATION OF ROTATIONS IF THE BALL IS SKIPPED AND THEN GOES TO THE CORNER—HIGH POST VACANT

If the ball has just been skipped from wing to wing and both guards and forwards have taken their correct rotations (Diagram 49), and then it is passed to the wing either by the low post (O4) stepping out or by O5 overloading to the corner, then the following rotation occurs:

Diagram 49   **Diagram 50**

X1
- Sinks toward the ball and stays on the line and up the line with O1, but is ready to take anyone cutting into the high post

X2
- Stays with O2 and moves into a denial position so as not to let the ball out of the box in the corner

X3
- Sinks with the ball and stays on line with O3, ready to help on the low post being fronted

X4
- Closes out on the man in the corner with high hands, forcing him baseline

X5
- Bumps X4 to the corner and fronts the low post

GUARD ROTATION ON DRIBBLE PENETRATION FROM THE WING—HELP SITUATION

General rules on dribble penetration:

- A dribble down is like a pass—it shortens the box

- Dribble penetration pulls the guards deeper into the box

- The guards follow the same rotations on high post coverage; if one leaves, the other must come into the high post

Diagram 51

X1
- Moves as the ball is dribbled deeper into the box

- Dives into the high post to intercept the pass going away from the basket

- Reads the strength of the double team and anticipates the pass out

- Blocks out man in the high post on a shot

X2
- Moves with the dribbler and has low post coverage if X5 steps out to help early

- Must dive in front of the low post and look for a bounce pass

- Has ball-side low post block-out on a shot

FORWARD ROTATION ON DRIBBLE PENETRATION FROM THE WING—HELP SITUATION

General rules on dribble penetration:

- Since we are inviting dribble penetration to the baseline, we must expect it

- The defender on the post helps early

- He traps with the wing on the low side with his hands high

Diagram 52

X3
- Forces the ball to the baseline, and as the dribbler goes in that direction, he traps with X5

- Traps on the high side with hands high, obstructing vision

X4
- Anchors the defense on the weak side

- Takes away the crosscourt pass under the basket, where the dribbler will look first

- Rebounds weakside

- If X2 is slow to drop into the low post and the post receives the ball, doubles the low post with X2

X5
- Helps early and shuts off the baseline, trapping on the low side with X3

- Attacks with high hands to take away the lob and obstruct the offensive player's vision

COMBINING THE ROTATIONS OF THE GUARDS AND THE FORWARDS ON DRIBBLE PENETRATION FROM THE WING—HELP SITUATION

Diagram 53

X1
- Drops from denying the point reversal to the high post and anticipates the pass out of the trap

X2
- Moves down with the dribbler and dives in front of the low post player

X3
- Stays with the dribbler and traps on the high side with X5

X4
- Anchors the weak side, ready to help on the low post and rebound opposite

X5
- Helps early and traps on the low side with X3

KEYS FOR BOTH GUARDS AND FORWARDS THAT CAN MAKE A BIG DIFFERENCE IN THE SUCCESS OF THIS MATCHUP:

- All defensive players must anticipate and be ready to move while the ball is traveling in the air to the next location.

- It is essential that the first player to get to the ball stay with the ball, and the other players will match up around him.

- A defender on the ball should never leave a dribbler without "releasing or bumping him" onto another defender.

- Just as in our man-to-man defense, every defender must keep his head on a swivel to be able to see both the ball and the offensive player he is matched up with, while staying on the line and up the line.

- The defender should use his man-to-man techniques to defend a cutter until he can "release" him or pass him to another defender.

- The defender on the ball must keep pressure on the ball and obstruct his vision.

- Defenders on the ball and away from the ball must keep the ball out of the middle of the court. They must be able to prevent dribble penetration toward the middle by forcing baseline and must be able to deny entry passes that allow the ball to be caught in the middle of the defense.

- The guards and the forwards must work together to keep the ball out of the high post area. This defense is the most vulnerable when the ball is located in the high post because there is no box established.

- All players must work to continually take away the vision of the offensive players as much as possible.

- A penetrating dribble toward the baseline is treated the same as a pass, and all defenders must make the appropriate adjustments.

- It is always a five-on-five game, and each defender should always have a man to check and should not get caught guarding a spot on the floor.

REMINDERS THAT ARE ESSENTIAL FOR SOUND GUARD PLAY IN THIS MATCHUP:

- The point defender has to work constantly to keep the ball out of the center of the floor so that we can establish a box on one side of the floor.

- Each guard must control the dribbler so that he keeps the ball from penetrating the center of the floor.

- If the ball is thrown toward the basket, over the guard's head, he must seek the level of the ball and dig down for the ball.

- We encourage our defenders not to slap at the ball, but rather to attempt to grab it out of the offensive player's hands.

- If guards are tipping at the ball, they should tip up at the ball and not slap down on it.

- The guards cannot defend air or a spot on the floor. They must rotate to find a man and then establish the proper on-the-line, up-the-line position to keep the ball from coming out of the box.

- If no offensive man is in the defender's area, the guards must locate and match up with the next man over.

- This defense is an aggressive attacking defense and must be played that way by active and aggressive guards.

- The guard positions are interchangeable and must be able to communicate as they exchange assignments.

REMINDERS THAT ARE ESSENTIAL FOR SOUND FORWARD PLAY IN THIS MATCHUP:

- Forwards should check all perimeter and post players with high hands to obstruct their vision and their ability to make quick passes or reads.

- As the forwards close out on the perimeter, the amount of pressure they apply will depend on the abilities of the offensive player and their own quickness relative to the offensive man's.

- Forwards should attempt to make wing players dribble the ball toward the baseline so they can shorten the box.

- Forwards should attempt to make post players dribble the ball so we can dig down with our other defenders and disrupt their timing.

- All three back positions in this defense are interchangeable, and communicating with each other is required in order to be successful.

- Block-outs are made on the offensive player a defender is matched up with. Everyone will have an assigned man on each shot.

- Every time the ball is moved either by pass or dribble, the forwards must make the proper adjustment in positioning.

- One of the forwards is always anchored on the weak side so that the weakside rebound area is covered.

- Just like the guards, the forwards must be aggressive, actively moving defensive players.

- The forward must never overrun the basketball on either a closeout or a trap. This move is perhaps the dumbest defensive play in basketball.

CHAPTER 2

The 1-2-2 Matchup

THE 1-2-2 MATCHUP ZONE

Each year, as we are evaluating the personnel that we are going to playing with, we examine a variety of matchup zones to see if there is one alignment that will allow us to best utilize our talent. In years when we utilize three guards on offense and they are all tall and very active, we have installed the 1-2-2 matchup zone. It has been an effective change-up from the 1-1-3 and allows those three active players to get out and defend a lot of ground on the perimeter, to trap out front and to use the length of their arms to disrupt the spacing and timing of most zone offenses.

During the preseason, when we are deciding on which matchup to use, the decision is most often dependent on fitting our own players' talents. But occasionally, we will look at specific teams on our schedule that we must be able to defeat and then prepare a defense that eliminates their strengths. If the teams we must defeat to win a championship are teams that have great perimeter shooting and are not as strong in the post, then we include the 1-2-2 in our defensive scheme. Even though it may not be our primary defense, we will use it as a change-up to attempt to take away their area of strength and make them adjust their offense. The goal of any defense is to prevent scoring, so if adjusting our own alignment or zone front makes it more difficult to attack us, then it has been time well spent.

Matchup zones provide a great deal of flexibility for defensive coaches and often do not take that long to learn, especially if you utilize your man-to-man defensive rules and terminology. One of the keys to success for our multiple defenses is to keep our defensive concepts and principles as consistent as possible for our athletes, regardless of which type of defense we are playing. Our primary defensive goals do not change, regardless of the type of matchup zone we choose to play. We are still trying to accomplish the following objectives:

- Force the offensive players to play outside their normal spacing

- Defend only a portion of the court by forcing the offense into a smaller and smaller box

- Keep the ball out of the high post area

- Deny penetration to the middle of the floor

- Deny any penetrating passes to the middle of the floor

- Deny all straight-line cuts to the basket

- Make weakside cutters coming toward the ball run through an obstacle course, and get physical contact with them to prevent any straight cuts with defenders trailing the cutter

- Provide opportunities to trap

- Provide strong rebounding position, especially on the weak side, to prevent second-chance opportunities for your opponent

- Be able to challenge and contest good perimeter shooters

GENERAL ALIGNMENT OF THE 1-2-2 MATCHUP ZONE

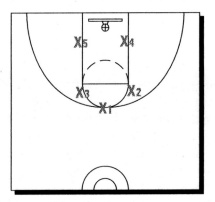

Diagram 54

Diagram 54 shows the basic alignment of the 1-2-2 matchup zone. Our personnel initially line up in these spots and, as with our other matchup zones, they must know who they are guarding and also be able to communicate with their teammates. As the game begins, you show your matchup to your opponents and then see how they have prepared themselves to attack it. They will usually have a specific offensive formation that they have practiced to contend with your alignment.

After you have seen how your opponents are going to attack the 1-2-2 alignment, you may make small adjustments that are predicated on their personnel or initial cuts. The offensive formation that your opponents employ will not defeat your matchup; their cuts, screens and player movement will be the things that you must be able to defend once the game is under way. Your players must be prepared to use their individual defensive fundamentals to neutralize the variety of offensive maneuvers they may see. Your coaching staff needs to be able to adjust during the game to take away offensive movement that has proven to be effective.

Most zone offenses include one of the following principles: overload, isolation, screening, gapping or free-lance. Once you have determined which style of offense your opponent favors, it becomes the objective of the defense and the coaching staff to take away the strengths of that offense and make the offensive players alter their attack.

As discussed earlier, we often will choose the 1-2-2 alignment when we have three tall and active perimeter defenders. If we have only two tall front players and one short one, we will use the tall players on the wing and the short player on the point. If we have only one tall perimeter defender and two shorter ones, then we will most likely use the one tall player at the point. Occasionally, we may place our best perimeter defender of the three in the area where we anticipate the opponent's strongest shooter to play. If the strength of the opposing team is dribble penetration by a specific player, then we may choose to match up our best on-the-ball defender to the area of the floor where that offensive player operates. Having the versatility to move your top personnel to match up and eliminate the strengths of your opponent is a huge factor in the success of this defense.

If you make the choice to play this matchup, you must also have two bigger players capable of becoming good post defenders who can match up with the offensive posts you are going to have to play against. If you have only one player who fits this description, then you may be better off choosing a 1-3-1 alignment. The two baseline defenders need to be able to cover both low and high post areas, and you will depend on them to carry most of the rebounding responsibilities. If one of the two lower defenders defends the high post or low post better than the other one, it would be wise to prioritize their coverage in case you have to cover a high-low offensive attack. In the diagrams in this chapter, we will designate X5 as the player who is the stronger defender in the high post, and X4 as the remaining matcher.

MATCHUP RULES FOR THE TOP DEFENDERS

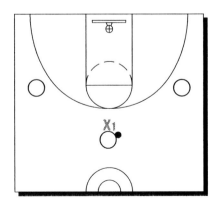

Diagram 55

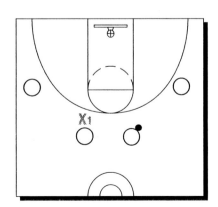

Diagram 56

X1 is the defender who all the other defenders key off of for their initial coverage. The other four defenders must be able to see him as the ball is brought into the offensive end of the court.

X1 will check the offensive player in the point alley of the court when he has the ball (Diagram 55). Diagram 56 shows his matchup when the ball is brought into the offense by a two-guard front. In this case, he checks the player offset to the right, whether he has the ball or not.

X1 must have quick lateral movement that allows him to cut off dribble penetration, pressure the ball to take away vision and force the offensive point man out of the center of the court so we can establish a defensive box. He has to be able to take away ball reversal by staying on the line, up the line with the offensive point player. Taking away ball reversal will slow the offense and force the ball further into the box, which is to the advantage of the defense. There will be times when it is necessary for X1 to dive to the high post area after his man has entered the ball. As he does this, he must begin to identify his next matchup responsibility.

X2 matches up and covers the first offensive player to the left of X1. Diagrams 57, 58 and 59 provide some examples of who X2 would match up with, depending on who is the first man to the left of X1. X2 needs to be the next-quickest defender on the perimeter and has many of the same defensive responsibilities as X1. None of the three top defenders can allow dribble penetration to the center of the floor, and they all need to work together to seal the gaps between them.

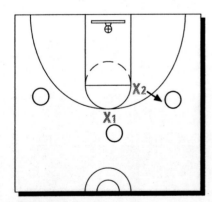

Diagram 57

Diagram 58

Diagram 59

X3 is the third wing defender and matches up to cover the first offensive player to the right of the player checked by X1. Since most teams attack the right side of the court, you may want to place either the weakest defender of the three or the strongest rebounder of the three top players in this position. Diagrams 60, 61 and 62 show initial coverages for X3 as he reads and reacts to the matchup of X1.

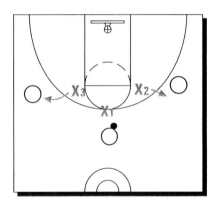

Diagram 60

Diagram 61

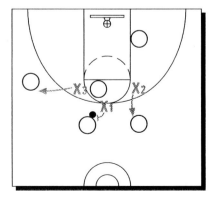

Diagram 62

MATCHUP RULES FOR BASELINE DEFENDERS IN THE 1-2-2

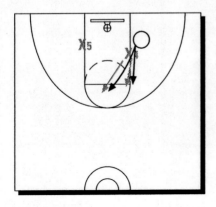

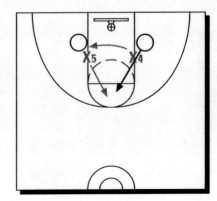

Diagram 63   **Diagram 64**

As discussed earlier in this chapter, X4 and X5 can be utilized in several ways. Their responsibilities are tied to their athletic ability. If they are equal in their ability to defend high and low, then you can have them simply divide the court in half and have them cover the post men, who may flash on their side. If one of them has an athletic advantage over the other, then that player can cover the high post, regardless of the direction the cutter comes from. Diagram 63 demonstrates coverage of equal players covering their side, while Diagram 64 shows X5 as the more advanced or active defender, who has responsibility for the first cutter into the high post, no matter where he originated from. In this case, X4 must be prepared to move across the lane or wherever it is required that he move to check to the offensive low post. It is preferable, especially with younger players, to let each low defender cover, as if he is an equal.

X4 has the coverage responsibility for the second offensive player to the left of X1 (Diagram 65). X5 follows the key established when X1 matches up and checks the second offensive player to the right of X1 (Diagram 66). If there is no second offensive player to the left or right of X1, then the defender (either X4 or X5, whose area is vacant) has got any player located in the high post (Diagram 67). Normally, there is no second player to the right or the left when teams initiate their offense in a 1-3-1 set. If the offensive team aligns in a 1-4 high set, both baseline defenders will cover the high post (Diagram 68). Both baseline defenders need to be aware of the movement and coverage of the other and need to communicate to help them anticipate the next cut or pass that the offensive team may make.

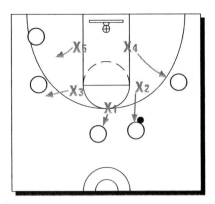

Diagram 65

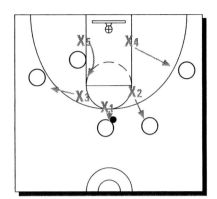

Diagram 66

Diagram 67

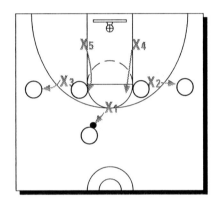

Diagram 68

MATCHING UP THE 1-2-2 AGAINST OVERLOADS

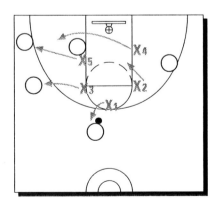

Diagram 69

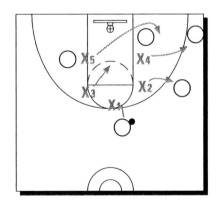

Diagram 70

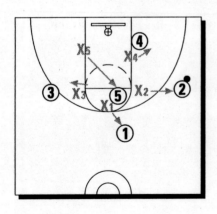

Diagram 71

Diagram 72

From time to time, you will face teams that immediately align themselves in an "overload" set. This set essentially means that they attempt to place more players in one area of the floor than you have the ability to cover. This strategy causes a standard zone defense to be distorted and out of its normal areas of coverage; but for the matchup, it is just a matter of locating and matching up with the offensive player you are responsible for based on our keys.

The only adjustment that needs to take place is for X4 to take the third player to the right of X1 (a low post player counts as a perimeter player) if the overload is to his right, and X5 would make that rotation if the overload is to the left of X1. In Diagram 69, the overload is to the right of X1. In Diagram 70, the overload is to the left of X1, causing X4 to go to corner coverage and X5 to take the third man to the left of X1, who happens to be the low post player.

If your baseline players do not have equal coverage ability, or if you have one dominant rebounder whom you do not want to have corner coverage, you can assign one of them to go to the corner, regardless of which side, and the other one to cover the low post. This maneuver would strengthen your defense by allowing each player to perform in areas where they can be successful.

When teams overload and occupy the high post or mid-post areas, it results in additional thinking—especially by the two baseline defenders—and additional responsibilities by the wings. Diagram 71 illustrates the coverage against a standard high post overload. Defenders follow their basic keys and match up. Diagram 72 offers a new situation, where there are no offensive players to the right side of X1 and there is a player in the corner (O3) and a player in the "short corner" (O4), as well as the mid-post (O5). The baseline defenders have the best view of the alignment and should alert the weakside wing (X3) that they are going to need help in the mid-post or high post area. X3 should also quickly see that there are no offensive players on his half of the court and all is "clear." This call allows the baseline defenders to stay low and match up with the corner and the short corner and for X3 to slide into the high post or mid-post area and take that coverage responsibility. Depending on your personnel, you could lock X5 on anyone in the high post in every circumstance, which would require X3 to rotate all the way to the short corner.

PRACTICING INITIAL COVERAGES IN THE 1-2-2 MATCHUP

Diagram 73

Diagram 74

As a coach of the matchup, you have to be able to anticipate how opponents are going to try to attack your 1-2-2 alignment. You should therefore practice having an offensive team bring the ball into half court against your basic 1-2-2 and then set up in the formations you anticipate seeing and make sure that all five defenders can successfully make the correct decisions about their initial coverage. Until they can make those decisions, it doesn't make any sense to start covering ball or player movement.

Most teams will initially place two guards on top to split X1. Therefore, in most cases, your players are going to have to be able to match up against both 2-1-2 (2-3) and 2-2-1 formations. Diagrams 73 and 74 demonstrate the proper coverages against these two offensive sets. Following the keys in diagram 73, when there are two guards, X1 matches up with the one on the right side, whether he has the ball or not (O1). X2 takes the first player on the perimeter to the left (O2) of X1. X3 takes the first player on the perimeter to the right of X1 (O4). X4 will be assigned to the second player to the left (O3), and X5 checks the high post. Diagram 74 shows the coverage against a 2-2-1 alignment as X1 matches up.

ROTATION AND COVERAGE ON DRIBBLE PENETRATION IN THE 1-2-2 MATCHUP

Diagram 75

Regardless of how talented your perimeter defenders are, there will be times when they get beaten off the dribble. In most cases, the adjoining perimeter player will stop dribble penetration by "sealing the gap." The sealing-the-gap techniques will be discussed in the chapter on matchup fundamentals.

When a dribbler splits the perimeter defenders and gets into the middle of the defense, it can cause extreme difficulties for your defense. Too often, this action will result in a baseline defender coming to help and the ball getting dropped off for a lay-in, or eventually foul trouble for the baseline defenders. In order to be prepared for this situation against your 1-2-2, it is essential that you practice how you want your players to rotate to cover dribble penetration.

Diagram 75 shows the rotation we want our team to use when the perimeter defenders are beaten. The players are already matched up when X1 is beaten off the dribble and X2 does not seal the gap. Our weakside baseline defender (X5) is responsible for stopping the dribbler and is looking to take a charge. Our weakside perimeter defender (X3) must drop to the basket area and get into the passing lane of the lowest offensive player on his side (O4). Both players can recover to their original assignment if X1 can gain control of the dribbler or if O1 kicks the ball out to O3. The final thing we do not want to give up on dribble penetration is a pass back to the perimeter for a shot.

CHAPTER 3

Drilling the Fundamentals of the Matchup

OVERVIEW

Drills for the matchup defenses are essential for team success. Some of the drills we use require an understanding of the principles we use for man-to-man, while others are specific to our matchup rules. Drilling individual fundamentals with consistent repetitions helps to increase each player's confidence in his ability to accomplish his responsibilities at the moment of truth. As the self-confidence of individual players grows, the confidence of the team will show up in the overall defensive scheme. A coach cannot expect his defense to be sound unless he has covered every possibility that his individual players have to be able to stop, and his players have proven in practice that they understand and can execute the techniques necessary to do their part within the team defense.

If you are going to play the matchup, it is necessary to scout your opponent' offensive movements. This preparation will help you to devise drills that simulate their initial alignments and cuts. Once you have identified how they are going to attack your defense, the coaching staff must break down each movement into drill form and allow the individual players to successfully defend them before putting the whole team defense together. Do not expect your players to be able to carry over into a game those skills they have not physically been able to perform in practice. The preparation you give your players should take all the questions out of their minds and allow them to be confident that they can stop anything the other team may throw at them.

Most of the work for the coaching staff will be done before you step on the practice floor. You should devise drills that are relevant and exacting so that, when your players come to practice, their time and energies will be directed toward drills that will accomplish exactly what they are going to have to face in game situations.

INDIVIDUAL CLOSEOUTS

Diagram 76

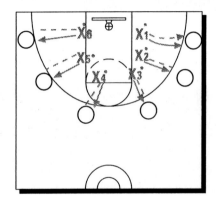

Diagram 77

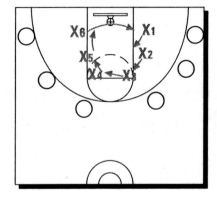

Diagram 78

Every player must be able to close out correctly so that the ball handler is controlled and channeled in the direction the defender chooses. Using principles similar to our man principles, the defender is trying to force the offensive player further into a box so the team doesn't have as much of the floor to defend. Players closing out on the ball need to keep their inside foot forward and place both feet in such a way that they push the dribble to the baseline. Diagram 76 shows the feet of on-the-ball defenders in various locations on the floor.

Diagram 77 shows how we would practice this closeout skill with 12 players at once. Each defender (X1–X6) will start with a basketball and throw a one-hop pass to the offensive player he is going to close out on. He then uses a controlled speed to shorten the distance. If he goes too slowly, the offensive player can get an uncontested shot. If he goes too quickly, too high or out of control, the offensive player can beat him with a drive. The first responsibility of the defender is not to get beaten on a drive.

We will rotate the players around the horn to allow them to be able to close out correctly in any area of the floor. Diagram 78 shows this rotation. After each player has been in every spot on the floor, we change offense to defense and continue. This drill can be done in a short amount of time and still get the defenders enough repetitions that the closeout skill becomes habit.

DEFENDING THE DRIBBLER

Diagram 79

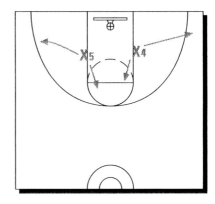

Diagram 80

Dribble penetration will kill any defense because it puts all the defenders in either a help or a rotation situation. In order to stop dribble penetration, each defender must be accomplished at controlling the ball after taking a correct closeout. By identifying what areas of the court each defender is going to have to be able to check the ball in, set up your drills to place each player in those spots on the court where he is going to have to be able to cut off and control the dribbler. The perimeter players have to be able to close out and control mainly in the top half of the court and on the wings. The baseline defenders are going to have to close out and control mainly in the high post and the corners.

Diagram 79 shows where we would focus the attention of defenders X1, X2 and X3 in a closeout and control-the-dribbler drill, if we were playing the 1-2-2 matchup.

Diagram 80 shows the areas of the floor where we should focus our attention for the baseline defenders.

SEAL THE GAP DRILL

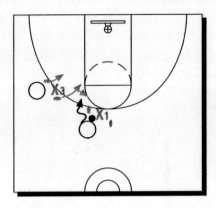

Diagram 81

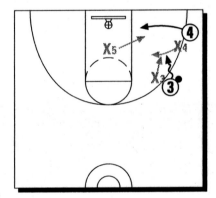

Diagram 82   **Diagram 83**

In order to stop dribble penetration, it is often necessary to require the help of the teammate next to you. This is called "sealing the gap." In man-to-man, who the next defender is changes constantly. In the matchup, the majority of the time, it is the same person on your right and left. We work hard to coordinate the timing and techniques between two defenders to cut off the driver and not let the ball get into the center of the defense. We hope that in most cases each individual defender can control his offensive opponent by himself, but when help is needed, we have to have all the potential gaps in the defense closed, even if it requires two defenders.

The top defender in the 1-2-2 needs to be able to seal with the two wings, and the wings need to work with each other and the baseline defenders. All players need this skill, and it can be practiced in all areas of the court. In Diagram 81, we illustrate with dots the position of the feet of the defender on the ball and the defender off the ball, who will have to come and seal the gap. In this case, X3 is in an on-the-line, up-the-line stance and simply has to swing his top foot back and then quickly slide to the gap with his whole body. Too often, defenders will only get to the gap with their hands, and reaching will not only not stop the driver, but it will also get us into foul trouble.

If the defender who is sealing the gap sees that the on-the-ball defender has controlled the dribbler by himself, he can recover back to his offensive assignment. We call this "seal and recover." As we set up the drills to practice this skill, we allow either offensive player to attempt to split the gap with the dribble, which makes either defender responsible for sealing and recovering.

In Diagram 82, we show how we would drill sealing the gap with X3 and X4 in a normal matchup alignment. As O3 penetrates the gap, X3 attempts to stop him by himself. X4 reads the dribbler and sees if X3 needs help to seal the gap. If he does not, X4 stays matched in an on-the-line, up-the-line position. If X3 cannot keep the dribbler out of the gap, X4 hedges off with the correct footwork and then recovers back to his man when O3 is controlled or when O3 passes the ball to O4.

Diagram 83 shows the same drill from the same location on the floor, but with X5 in a help position. When we add X5 into the drill, we will allow O4 to cut to the basket as X4 goes to seal. If O4 cuts to the basket, X5 will cover him, and when X4 recovers from sealing the gap, he must be prepared to identify his next matchup responsibility. We will continue to add offensive players so that X4 can read his key and locate the proper player to match up with.

RESPONSIBILITIES OF DEFENDERS OFF THE BALL IN THE 1-2-2 MATCHUP

The following list includes thoughts and techniques that our coaching staff will continually correct and reinforce to our matchup defenders when they are away from the ball:

- You must constantly communicate to your teammates, verbalizing to them your location, any potential player movement into their area, releasing of cutters, any help that may be required on dribble penetration, possible screens and whenever a shot is taken.

- Whenever you are next to the ball defender, be prepared to help seal the gap.

- Keep on the line and up the line and constantly turn your head to have vision of the ball and your matchup.

- Jam all cutters toward the ball to make them change their path.

- Stay in the correct on-the-line, up-the-line position when you are on the weak side and encourage the ball to go further into the box and not be allowed to be passed out of the box.

- Weakside defenders are the most important rebounders and defenders and must be ready to locate and block off any offensive player.

- Move while the ball is in the air on each pass in order to maintain correct positioning.

- When your man moves from the strong side to the weak side of the floor, release him and quickly relocate your new matchup.

- Think interception on every lazy pass or on any pass out of the box.

- Team defense continues until we have the ball.

COVERAGE FOR THE WEAKSIDE DEFENDERS IN THE 1-2-2 MATCHUP

Diagram 84

Diagram 85

Defending off the ball is often more difficult than defending on the ball. The on-the-ball defender has to have the necessary physical skills and footwork to stop the dribbler, but the off-the-ball defender is responsible for his matchup, as well as changing his matchup and helping on the ball.

First, I am going to discuss the techniques necessary to contain the ball with weakside positioning and then get into the techniques for cutters toward the ball and away from the ball.

In order to drill our positioning, we will begin with the five offensive players stationary and move the ball around the perimeter. Normally, we are not going to allow the ball to be reversed or taken further out of the box, but in this drill we are working on each player adjusting his position and not worrying about stealing the ball. Often, we will ask our players to play with their hands and feet in the correct position, but not touch the ball as it is moved around the perimeter.

Diagram 84 shows the alignment we may practice against if our next opponent uses a single-post and four-perimeter-player attack. Each defender must not only match up as the offensive team comes down the court, but also position themselves according to their strongside or weakside position.

Diagram 85 shows the adjustment required by the weakside defenders on a single pass by the offensive team, even if no offensive players change their location. As O1 passes to O3, X1, X2, X4 and X5 all must move as the ball is in the air. They must be in correct position with both their hands and feet to deny a direct pass, a weakside to strongside cut, and to be within a step of the newly established box.

We will continue to move the ball without moving any offensive players until we are confident that all five defenders understand correct positioning as the ball is swung. We will also bring our offensive team down the floor and set up in any formation that we anticipate our opponents may show us. Matching up and moving with each pass to a new position is easy, as long as the players are not moving. Movement by the offensive players not only requires additional adjustment of positioning, but also changing who you are matched up with. In the next section, we will begin adding player movement and defending cuts toward the ball and away from the ball. Most of our man-to-man principles and terms apply when we are denying and jamming cutters.

DEFENDING CUTTERS GOING TOWARD THE WEAK SIDE

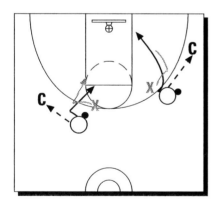

Diagram 86

Diagram 87

As an offensive player leaves the ball side of the court and goes into the key area, our matchup defender must be able to stay with him long enough to deny him from receiving a pass on the way to the basket. Our defender then needs to release him in time to recover to any potential new assignment.

Diagram 86 shows the first drill we use to defend this kind of a cut. As the offensive player passes the ball to the coach in the corner, the defender must quickly accomplish the following techniques:

- Jump to the ball so that the cutter cannot receive a quick return pass.

- Change his stance from influencing toward the baseline to denying the pass.

- Sink toward the basket so he cannot be back cut.

- Still be ready to seal the gap.

- Physically body check and jam the cutter to get him to change his path and to disrupt any offensive timing.

- Be prepared to release and quickly return to the perimeter to prevent an uncontested shot by any new matchup.

After the defender can successfully defend the first few steps of the cutter leaving the strong side of the court, he must be able to release or pass the cutter to a teammate and then recover to a new assignment. Diagram 87 shows a drill we use to accomplish this goal. A common offensive strategy is to pass the ball into the corner and then cut through the heart of the defense as the offensive perimeter players rotate toward the ball. In this diagram, X3 will use the technique from the previous drill and then add in the release and recovery he is going to have to be able to do in order to successfully play the 1-2-2 matchup.

We will take the cutter as deep as the edge of the key if necessary before we release him and recover to O1, who is filling the area vacated by O3. The sooner X4 can call release and make the exchange with X3, the easier it is for X3 to return to the perimeter. As X4 receives his new assignment, he must immediately assume a position in the passing lane and keep vision. Next, he begins the process of adjusting his new weakside position and preparing for other cutters or passes which will change his responsibilities. This type of drill can be created for any area of the court or for any specific cuts that your opponents may run.

The techniques of this fundamental will not change, for either the defender passing the cutter or the defender receiving the cutter. Each player must anticipate the release and recovery part of the exchange. The weakside defenders, who will normally be receiving the cutters, need to understand that they are the ones with the best vision of the whole play as it develops. Therefore, they must be the ones responsible for verbally alerting their teammate to exchange before it even happens.

DEFENDING CUTTERS GOING TOWARD THE STRONG SIDE

Diagram 88

Diagram 89

Diagram 90

Diagram 91

Diagram 92

Cutters going from the strong side to the weak side are potential receivers for the first few steps as they cut to the basket; but once they get to the weak side, the only pass they can receive is a skip pass. Cutters moving from the weak side toward the ball are much more of a potential threat to score. Any cuts toward the ball must be defended to prevent the ball from being caught in the middle of the defense. Putting extreme pressure on the ball and reducing the passer's vision can really help passing and receiving the cutter from a weakside defender to a strongside defender.

All gaps must be protected, and the cutter must be made to run through an obstacle course to get to the ball side. Just as in the man-to-man defense, we cannot trail a cutter moving toward the ball. By having your defenders in the correct off-the-ball position, it makes it easier to jam the cutter and verbalize to your teammates when you are making an exchange. Perimeter and baseline players need to be able to pass and immediately recover to the new matchup.

The following diagrams provide some examples of passing and receiving cutters coming toward the strong side of the court. Obviously, we cannot cover every type of cut alignment you may see. But if you and your coaching staff are able to identify the type of cuts each team will most likely run against your defense, and then break those cuts into game-like drills, your players will have more success carrying those defensive techniques over to the game.

Diagram 88 is an example of a weakside guard cutting from the perimeter on top and cutting to the strongside corner to create an overload. Defenders have already matched up off the key established by X1. As O1 cuts down on the weak side, X5 is aware of his movement and knows he must match up with him if he goes toward the strong side of the court. X5 calls "release" as O1 moves to the ball-side corner and matches with him. X3 stays in an on-the-line, up-the-line position according to the position of the ball and the ball being received by O3.

In Diagram 89, X1 has matched with O1, who has the ball. A weakside wing, O3, cuts toward the strong side of the court and can either stop on the block or go all the way through to the strongside corner. X4 drops back with him and can stay with the cutter if X5 is the baseline defender assigned to stay on the high post. If the two baseline defenders are equal and can exchange jobs, then X4 drops with the cutter and releases to X5, who covers the block or the corner with O3. X4 should recover to the high post player. Just as in man-to-man, you have to assess the strengths of your own defenders in order to allow them to be successful.

Diagram 90 illustrates defending a cutter moving across the baseline in a move similar to a flex cut. X5 calls "release" and takes the cutter, beating him across the key to the block. Diagram 91 shows the same switch if the cutter is going to the high post. X4 jams the cutter as he comes over the top of O5 and then releases him to X5 and slides into a position to deny the ball to O5 on the low block. X5 anticipates the cut and calls "release" to X4. He then jams the cutter, taking away a direct-line cut to the ball and not letting him get to the high post without changing his path.

Diagram 92 illustrates a weakside-to-strongside cut with no offensive high post players in the initial set. This cut from this set will require two different passes. X2 drops with the cutter and releases to X4. X4 denies the pass across the key and then passes O2 to X5, who covers the corner.

DEFENDING MULTIPLE CUTS FROM THE SAME SET

Diagram 93

Diagram 94

The next principle of defending cutters in the matchup involves more than one cutter. Diagram 93 shows O2 cutting from strong side to weak side and O5 cutting from weak side toward the ball. X2 releases to X5. X5 releases to X3. X3 releases to X1.

Diagram 94 shows the matchup defending two different types of cuts. O2 hits the corner and goes away. O3 flashes into the middle and then goes to the ball-side block. O1 follows the ball toward the corner and looks for a return pass out of the corner. Defensively, X2 drops with the first cutter and then must recover in time to prevent the ball from being passed out of the corner. O2 is briefly released to X5, and then X3 releases O3 to X5 and covers O5 on the weakside low post. X5 has O3 on the ball-side block. X1 must drop into the middle of the key and locate the unguarded player on the weak side (O2) and get into a pistols position.

As your players become more and more comfortable with multiple cuts and ball movement, begin to introduce them to the pattern offense that they will be seeing from the next opponent. Allow them to defend the offense at a walking speed, practicing all the exchanges and calls necessary to correctly defend each move and to build confidence. Gradually speed up the offense. With each practice session, your defenders should become more confident with their ability to stop any offensive movement they may encounter.

CHAPTER 4

Making Adjustments from Your Matchup Zone

OVERVIEW

One of the goals of any defensive coach is to confuse and disrupt the offensive team. As an offensive team gets comfortable with a particular defense, you may be forced to make adjustments to keep them off balance. These small adjustments can prove very effective for your team. Plus, they don't take long to teach and learn.

Sometimes an adjustment can be as simple as changing a single defensive player; at other times, it may be involve changing and playing an entirely different defense. Good defenses should control the action, and if you find that yours is reacting and not dictating, then it may be time to make an adjustment. Just as a good pitcher in baseball can keep a hitter off balance by changing speeds and pitches, your defense can keep the offensive team away from its strengths and keep it constantly guessing.

If you can make the other team change its normal offensive patterns or cause confusion even for a few possessions, you may be able to change the outcome of the game. In basketball, confusion spells defeat. Controlling a team's offense doesn't mean that you have to record a shutout; it merely means that you force them to take shots that they do not normally take or make passes at a distance longer than they normally do. Variations or adjustments can be a surprise factor or can identify an area that your opponent is not prepared for. Adjusting can also become a challenge or a source of pride for your team.

Changing or adjusting your defenses can happen at any time during a game or a season. Therefore, you should continue to evaluate your personnel during the season and not be afraid to make changes that will give you an advantage.

BASIC REASONS FOR MAKING DEFENSIVE ADJUSTMENTS:

- When an offensive team is working at a speed that it practices

- When a team is operating at the spacing that it practices

- Before a team is comfortable with the defense you are playing

- When one individual is not able to handle a key matchup

- To double an outstanding individual player

- To speed up the tempo

- To slow down the tempo

- To force time-outs

- To create confusion

- To protect specific players of yours

TIMES DURING THE GAME TO MAKE ADJUSTMENTS:

- During any free throw situation

- After a made field goal

- After a time-out, especially when the time-out was taken to combat the defense you were in before the time-out

- After halftime

- Sideline out-of-bounds situations

- End out-of-bounds situations

- Behind near the end of a game

- Ahead near the end of a game

- When the opponent's point guard doesn't recognize defensive changes well

IF YOU WANT YOUR OPPONENT TO RUN ITS MAN OFFENSE AGAINST YOUR MATCHUP:

If for some reason you want to make your opponent run its man-to-man offense against your matchup, there are several methods you can use to accomplish this goal. The simplest method could be to have your man matched up on the basketball or the first cutter to follow that cutter and stay matched with him.

IF YOU WANT TO SLOW DOWN OFFENSIVE MOVEMENT:

If a team is running an offense that uses a great deal of player movement against your matchup, and you are having trouble staying with all the cuts, you can go to a standard zone. You can shift into the standard zone on a verbal call from the point

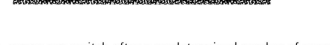

or from the bench, or you can switch after a predetermined number of passes. Often, after switching to a standard zone, it gives us a better picture of the pattern the offensive team is running against us, and we can make the necessary adjustments during a time-out or at halftime to get the correct coverage and go back to our matchup.

SWITCHING FROM OUR MATCHUP TO A STRAIGHT MAN-TO-MAN:

This change to a man-to-man may be the easiest and often the most effective of all the adjustments we can make during a game. If we are having trouble with certain cuts or matchups, we will occasionally make a quick transition to man-to-man out of our matchup zone. The best way is to match up on the first pass. Each player reads his keys, which will lead him to an assignment, and then they stay with that offensive player. We can also switch on a verbal call from our point man. If at some time we want to switch back while we are still on defense, we can do so when the player who keys our matchup is at the point and makes a verbal call.

Switching to man from your matchup can cause troubles for the offensive players. First, they see a zone look, and then when your defenders are matched up, you go into your basic man defense. We have found that many teams run their zone offense against our matchup and rely on quick ball movement and very little player movement. This is the perfect time to make the switch to man-to-man for a couple of possessions. Stationary offensive players are now being defended in a man-to-man defense. This move results in offensive players having to go higher and wider to get open and often forcing the player with the ball into a dribble situation because that is all that is available. As soon as the opposing players recognize that we are in a man-to-man and then start adding more offensive movement, we go back to our matchup or standard zone to neutralize their player movement.

SWITCHING DEFENSES ON EITHER A MADE OR A MISSED SHOT:

Diagram 95

Diagram 96

We have experimented with switching defenses on the basis of whether we score or not. This switching can be used on made or missed free throws or field goals. For example, we may play a man-to-man defense on misses, and a matchup on makes. This strategy is most effective against teams that have to take a little time to recognize what we are in and also against teams that have very different and specific offenses against the two different defenses. If nothing else, it may reduce the time they have remaining on the shot clock for that possession and cause either a hurried shot or a turnover.

Although the strategy to switch on a made free throw is employed by many teams for full-court pressing purposes, we feel that the element of surprise may even be a better way to disguise your half-court defense. Often, the element of surprise turns each possession into a guessing game for both the point guard and the opponent's bench, who are hard pressed to figure out which defense we are in. A small adjustment like this, which keeps the other team off balance, may be the thing that produces a run of a series of baskets for your team.

Diagram 95 is an example of a us showing a 1-2-2 against a team that initially lines up in a 2-1-2 set. On the first pass, we match up and go man-to-man. Each player reads his key off X1 and then closes out according to where the ball and his player are located.

Diagram 96 shows us beginning in the 1-2-2 matchup against an offensive set, and then staying man-to-man on the first pass. Each of these adjustments is extremely simple for our players to make after we have been playing the matchup, since it is the same thing they do to begin every defensive possession.

SWITCHING DEFENSES ACCORDING TO WHICH SIDE THE BALL IS ENTERED:

This method is another that prevents your opponent from knowing what defense you will be playing until the first pass. For example, we may play man-to-man whenever the ball is entered on our defensive right, and a matchup if it goes to our left. We will do this not only to confuse our opponents, but also depending on where they play their personnel. If they have an outstanding player on the right wing and enter the ball to him, we may want to be in our matchup if he drives or passes and cuts. We may want to be in man-to-man on his side if he is a great perimeter shooter and we want to deny his receiving the ball on the wing. If you do not want to wait until the first pass, then key which defense you are in by the side of the floor the ball is entered as it is dribbled over half court.

PLAYING A COMBINATION MATCHUP AGAINST A GREAT PERIMETER PLAYER:

This variation involves checking their outstanding player with a designated man-to-man defender and then having your other four defenders play either a diamond or a box matchup zone against the remaining four players. The person matching up man-to-man does not have to be your best defender. Often, it is more important to have your better defenders in the matchup zone part of the defense and give the individual defender lots of help. Even an average defender with some energy and intensity can stay with a single player if he doesn't have to focus on anything other than that person and his movement. When an opponent employs an unbalanced offensive game in the favor of one player, this strategy may prove effective against that opponent. Again, it comes down to your having four remaining players and your opponent having four players and being able always to be responsible for another man. If the man we are matching with is a point guard, then we will play a box; and if he is a wing, we will usually go to a diamond formation because those formations provide the most immediate help on the great player.

TIMES NOT TO SWITCH DEFENSES:

It is not always a good idea to make changes in your defense. If you have the better, stronger team, then in general, the fewer gimmicks you introduce, the better. Another time not to be changing defenses is when the change is more confusing to your team than your opponent. Confusion will not only allow easy baskets, but it will also discourage a team from being the aggressor. When you are evaluating your personnel, one of the most important keys is the overall intelligence of the team. Do not set your players up for failure by asking them to make adjustments that they cannot understand or will not be able to remember at the moment of truth. I have always felt it wasn't in our best interest to change whenever I had a team that was simply not playing hard. It was as if I were going to bail them out with a change-up instead of just getting them to play harder.

CHAPTER 5

Checklist to Evaluate Your Matchup

When you and your staff are evaluating the effectiveness of the matchup zone, it is important to keep a standard set of rules nearby to see where you need to make corrections or adjustments. The following thoughts are a checklist of reminders for your players and your coaches. You should identify the areas of weakness and correct those, rather than eliminate the whole defense.

- Prepare in practice all the cuts and movements that you anticipate your opponent will make.

- Force the opponent into a smaller and smaller area of the court.

- Force your opponent to score from the outside.

- Do not allow dribble or pass penetration to the middle of the floor.

- Overplay all dribblers to force them to the baseline—*pressure* the ball and *control* the ball.

- Take away the vision of the passer.

- Treat the dribble the same as a pass.

- Move, rotate and match up while the ball is in the air.

- Cutters going from the strong side to the weak side must be released in time for the perimeter player to return to the area he left so as not to allow the ball to be passed back out or give up an unguarded shot.

- Cutters coming from the weak side toward the ball must be made to go through an obstacle course—no direct cuts or trailing cutters.

- All defenders off the ball must maintain their vision and their spacing.

- Provide verbal cues that your players can use for communication with their teammates, and insist that these cues are used.

- Front all low post players and give weakside help.

- Anticipate and react to the next move by your matchup and by their whole team.

- Cover both strongside and weakside rebounding areas and block them out.

- Do not guard open space.

CONCLUSION

The matchup is not a zone and is not a man-to-man; it is the best of both defenses when played correctly. It should be a consistent one-on-one defensive situation, with the other four players using zone principles in the help positions. The matchup should take away offensive strategies of screening and cutting by passing the offensive players from defender to defender. We use all of our man-to-man principles and drills to teach the matchup. By applying these fundamentals, our defense should react without a lot of unnecessary thinking. Being a defense that anticipates and reacts instinctively is one of our team's strengths.

These matchup ideas are designed to be played aggressively and with great intensity—the harder the better. I sincerely hope this book helps to improve your understanding of matchup zones.

In closing, I would like to thank all my assistant coaches throughout my years of coaching for adding bits and pieces to this defense. They have all been great to work with. Also, I would like to thank John Hamel, our assistant sports information director, for all of his help on this project. Without him, this project would not have been possible. Have a successful year and enjoy this great game of ours.

Bob Huggins is a proven success as a program-builder, recruiter, game strategist and motivator. He has demonstrated this in a myriad of ways since joining the University of Cincinnati in 1989.

Inheriting a team that was short on numbers, Huggins inspired his initial team to a post season tournament and has done so every year since. Coach Huggins has compiled an impressive 247-82 record in his first 10 years at Cincinnati, making him the winningest coach in U. C. history.

For his efforts, Coach Huggins has been awarded many coaching honors, including the Ray Meyer Award as the Conference USA Coach of the Year in 1997 and 1998. He was also Basketball Times' selection for national coach of the year in 1997–'98, and was Playboy magazine's national coach of the year in 1992-'93.

Huggins began his coaching career as a graduate assistant at his alma mater, The University of West Virginia, in 1997. Subsequent coaching stints have included Ohio State (1978–'80), Walsh College (1980–'83), Central Florida (1983), and the University of Akron (1984–'89).

Born in Morgantown, W. Va., Huggins grew up in Gnadenhutten, Ohio where he played high school basketball for his father, Charles Huggins, at Gnadenhutten Indian Valley South. Bob and his wife, June, have two daughters, Jenna and Jacqueline.